~~~~~~ ~vernors

What Governors *Need to Know 2*

Jeff Jones   ✔ KU-471-760

David Fulton Publishers
London

First published
David Fulton Publishers 19

Note: The right of the author to be identified as the author of this work has been asserted by him in accordance with the Copyright, Designs and Patents Act 1988.

Copyright © Jeff Jones

British Library Cataloguing in Publication Data

A catalogue record for this book is available from the British Library

ISBN 1-85346-264-0

Typeset by EXCEPT*detail* Ltd, Southport.
Printed in Great Britain by The Cromwell Press, Melksham.

Contents

	Foreword	iv
	Introduction to the Series	v
	Acknowledgements	vi
Chapter 1	Finance and Budgeting	1
Chapter 2	Appointing Staff	15
Chapter 3	Behaviour Management	24
Chapter 4	Special Educational Needs	43
	Glossary	64

Foreword

School governors form the largest army of volunteer, unpaid public servants in the country. There are some 300,000 of us in 25,000 schools, all wanting the best for 'our' school. All of us want to raise the standard of education to the highest possible level, given the limits of human, financial and material resources available.

Governing a school is all about making decisions and adopting policies to determine how the school will function and best meet the needs of the community and of the students, their teachers and the support staff who work there. Governors need to understand their roles and responsibilities – massively changed over recent years – and what legal, moral, and physical constraints are placed upon them. This series of books will assist greatly. Governors are not 'know-it-alls' and governing bodies are made up of people from all walks of life, the majority of whom may have had little contact with schools for many years – perhaps since they themselves left school. In short, they need training, support and advice in order to assist them to make the best possible decisions for their school.

Ideally, governors should have access to a comprehensive, accredited training programme, backed up by a resource bank of books and papers about good practice and problem-solving. Jeff Jones has added a very useful and practical guide on school government to the resources available. This should make our task of governing schools easier to understand and therefore more rewarding. I am pleased to be associated with it.

Peter G Morris
Chair of the National Association of Governors and Managers
May, 1993

Introduction to the Series

New responsibilities given to governing bodies through legislation mean that the role of governors has increased substantially over recent years. With these enlarged responsibilities has come an increase in the level of information and understanding which governors are expected to acquire. It is now crucial that governors have access to clear and relevant information to enable them to understand not only the legal framework which now operates, but also the professional issues which form the basis of what goes on in schools.

This series is a direct and practical response to the need to provide brief, informative and clearly understandable publications which support the work of governors. Each publication deals with key items of governors' responsibilities and provides a concise and accurate account not only of the legal framework but also the salient professional issues which arise.

There is no intention to substitute for the Statutory Regulations, the Non-Statutory Guidance or any other form of authoritative guidance offered by Local Education Authorities (LEAs), Diocesan Authorities, etc. Neither is it intended that the publications should be read in one go. Rather, it is hoped that governors will make use of these publications to support them in acquiring the *basic* information they may need in order to carry out their responsibilities effectively.

The reader will find some duplication of information within the book. This is deliberate in order that each chapter is free-standing and complete in itself, allowing hard-pressed governors to select and read only those chapters relevant to their needs at a particular time.

In such a rapidly-changing field, publications of this kind cannot be absolutely up-to-date. The situation changes almost daily, and in matters where practice must follow the very latest guidance, it will be for your professional colleagues – especially the Headteacher – to be informed of the current position. Nevertheless, it is the publisher's and the author's intention to update the texts frequently to maintain their usefulness as overviews for the guidance of new governors and to keep more experienced governors in touch with ongoing change.

Acknowledgements

Grateful thanks go to the following for their contributions and help in producing this publication:

Mr Rodney Braithwaite, Headteacher, Flyford Flavell First School, Worcester

Ms Gillian Tee, Deputy Principal Educational Psychologist, Hereford and Worcester LEA

Mrs Janet Fielding, Advisory Teacher, Hereford and Worcester LEA

Mrs Irene Punt, Special Education Support Team, Hereford and Worcester LEA

CHAPTER 1
Finance and Budgeting

1. Statutory background

All local education authority (LEA) maintained primary and secondary schools with 200 pupils or more on roll are required to have fully delegated budgets by April 1994 at the latest. LEAs are permitted to extend the Local Management of Schools (LMS) scheme to smaller schools and special schools earlier where there is demand. The qualifying number of pupils includes those under five, either full or part-time, who are on the register. Governing bodies of grant-maintained (GM) schools receive their funding direct from the Secretary of State.

When schools receive full delegation, the governing body decides how the budget is to be spent and it has to keep accurate accounts of spending. Governors are expected to work with the headteacher who normally has responsibility for day-to-day budgetary management. In the case of the small number of schools with no delegated budget, the governors receive a statement from the LEA of how much the school costs to run, decide how to spend 'capitation' money and provide accounts of how the money is spent.

Further guidance may be found in DES Circulars 7/88 and 7/91.

2. Allocation of funds to schools

Under Section 42 of the Education Reform Act (ERA) a local council of elected members provides an annual statement of planned expenditure in all schools covered by the approved scheme of local management. Each school, through Section 42, will receive details of its formula budget provision, which will also show what this represents as expenditure per pupil. Governors sometimes express concern that the expenditure per pupil in their school differs widely from other schools of the same type. However, these variations can occur for several reasons:

- Weightings for small schools where extra funding may be necessary per head to cover fixed costs e.g. rent/rates.
- Some school premises may be more expensive to run because of their age or design. Aided schools may receive a lower allocation for relevant maintenance.
- There could be wide differences in salary costs for the staff.
- Some schools are allowed relief from Unified Business Rates (UBR) (in the case of high schools, the reduced level of spending need can be very considerable).

Does this cover all of the school's necessary expenditure?

At present most councils allocate about 85 per cent of their education budget directly to schools; the school's management and governing body then have responsibility for how that money is spent. The remaining 15 per cent retained by the council is spent in a number of ways to benefit the schools: for example, special help for children with learning difficulties, school inspectors and curriculum advisers, child psychologists, outdoor education centres and central administrative support.

This latter support covers a wide number of duties (for example, administering salaries, legal and insurance matters, VAT) and will be dealt with by the school itself if it becomes grant maintained. All this retained expenditure by the local authority comes under the heading of 'excepted expenditure' and is not the responsibility of the governors, although they may be involved occasionally in negotiations for a share of this expenditure.

The above section has highlighted where your school's budget is coming from, why there are differentials between schools of similar size and what the statutory requirements for a school budget are.

3. Preparation and rationale

What will guide us in the management of our school finances?

The effectiveness of this management will be judged by the extent to which the school's resources, which include time, money and staff, are used to maximise the school's aims and objectives. It will also reflect the extent to which the school aligns its spending priorities with its educational priorities; the cost effectiveness of programmes, procedures and practices; and the quality of the educational outcomes which follow. Governors may wonder how they can set about preparing themselves to meet these criteria. What is certain is that governors will need to gain knowledge in certain background areas before they apply themselves to financial management.

What do I need to know before I become involved in budgeting?

Firstly, it must be emphasised that you do not need to be a trained accountant in order to help administer school finances. You do need common sense and a sound knowledge of what has happened in the school in the recent past, what is happening at present and what it is intended should happen in the future. Essentially, you need to apply this knowledge to the needs of the school, which can then be related to resources available and can influence decisions to be taken.

You will be greatly assisted, especially if you are a new governor, in gaining background knowledge of the school by:

- making yourself aware of the aims and objectives of the school (normally found in the school brochure);
- studying the current school development plan, and if possible the previous one, so that you have an idea of how resources have been used/purchased/replaced in the past, and in which areas it is planned to provide resources in the short- and medium-term future. Some decisions in schools have, for a number of reasons, to be made very quickly and finance is no exception. However, it is most important that major expenditure, certainly for a complete financial year, is planned in advance; the plan will almost certainly include a contingency for emergencies or reactive decisions, but probably 95 per cent of an annual expenditure should have been 'spoken for' in planning;
- discovering how decisions are made concerning the budget. How are resources allocated? Is the head responsible for all decision-making or do other members of staff or the governors have an input? Are the decisions arrived at or discussed in a finance sub-committee; with head and chairman; with the whole school staff; or is there some other management structure? It may be a combination of all these, but you, as a governor, should have a knowledge of the procedures;
- discussing with staff. This will give you a clearer idea as to who

4

has an involvement with the school's finances, and whether they understand the way in which resources are allocated. This is particularly important where it concerns staff resources since this is a most sensitive area. The budget affects the number of teaching staff, the number of part-time staff and the number of non-teaching staff who are employed in the school. It is easily the largest area of spending in the school (80 to 85 per cent of the budget), so that it is in this area that excess under or overspending can often be found;

- looking at the school budget print-out. This should be available at all times and gives a number of indications as to the present use of the budget. You may also ask to see a summary of the budget from the previous year which will help you to gain a picture of where the school has come from. You should then have an idea as to how budget spending is related to school planning;

- examining the latest audit of the school's accounts, if available. This may have included recommendations and/or requirements for the school, and you might wish to see how these have been followed up;

- looking for indications of additional income. Schools have initiated numerous money-raising schemes over the years, and there is widespread additional community use of school premises. It is useful in gaining your background information, for you to look at the amount of external income, its sources and the use to which it is being put. Those involved in raising income for schools sometimes become disenchanted when they have no clear targets for their efforts, or when they cannot ascertain how the fruits of their exertions have been used.

If you have managed to look at some of these issues then you should have a much clearer idea of the financing and resourcing of the school – you will be aware of why the school receives its budget, as well as a background knowledge of where it has been spent, and where it is planned to spend it in future. Now you are ready to look at some of the details of the school budget.

4. The school's income and expenditure budget

At least monthly the school should either receive or, in the case of GM schools, produce a financial statement showing planned and actual budget income and expenditure. This should be broken down under a number of headings which describe areas of expenditure. A few weeks prior to the start of the financial year schools and governors should have a clear idea as to the sum allocated to the budget for the coming year, based upon the requirements of Section 42. This may have been broken down into 'indicative' spending by the LEA, which indicates to the school roughly how much might be spent by the school under each heading. However, the tendency increasingly is for schools to begin planning with a lump sum and then allocate parts according to need and identified objectives. Planning can take a number of courses.

First, the school management must identify a Base Budget – in other words what are the unavoidable costs – salaries, for instance. The school development plan should be to the forefront at this stage. Targets for development/improvement/replacement can be related to the amount of money left when fixed costs have been allocated. Schools have been very cautious in the past in that on average between 2–5 per cent of their total budget has not been earmarked for any specific area, but has been retained as a 'contingency'. There is nothing inherently wrong with this policy – 'good housekeeping' – but a significant number of schools have built up a substantial contingency, sometimes deliberately and sometimes by chance. Governors and the school management, in their planning, must establish clearly why they wish to create a contingency and whether there is any intended use for it in the future. No school is 100 per cent resourced to its full satisfaction, so it is appropriate to comment that schools retaining an excessive contingency, without adequate reason, are denying their children much-needed resources – either human or material.

What are the budget headings and how much should be allocated to them?

Authorities and schools may vary slightly in their heading descriptions but basically they cover salaries and related staff costs; supplies of equipment and services; and the costs of maintenance, fuel and water.

A. SALARIES

Provision has to be made for:

- teachers – including heads;
- incentives/bonuses;
- supply teachers;
- support staff – clerical, technical;

- non-teaching assistants in classrooms (NTAs).

For most staff, these costs will be salaries plus 'on-costs' for super-annuation, National Insurance, etc. The total cost to the budget generally works out at approximately 80 per cent. This is a key area of the budget where, in times of economic stringency, the management may feel inclined to make savings. This could lead to an increased pupil/teacher ratio, or less support from non-teaching staff, or a policy of employing less experienced teachers because their salaries will be lower than those of more experienced teachers higher on the salary scale. In all these situations the governors must be guided by criteria such as:

- What is best for the school and the children in it?
- What can we really afford at this time?
- What will the budget be in the future? For example, will there be any significant increase or decrease in the number of children on roll?

Great care must be taken when employing teachers to relate the job needs to the school's needs and to the money available. It is worth remembering that all teachers will have annual increments and unless there is a massive turnover in teachers it will not be possible to use a policy of continually appointing the 'youngest' and therefore the 'cheapest' staff.

Incentives, bonuses and enhancements

At present schools are provided with amounts of money correspond-ing to special allowances, 'A', 'B', 'C' etc. The number of these depends upon the number of pupils on roll, the age of the children and any special circumstances applying to the school – for example, substantial ethnic minorities, social priority areas, etc. Traditionally, these allowances have remained with the postholder, often without review, for as long as the holder remains at the school. However, some schools are now looking at incentives in a different light.

Several ingenious methods have been used to distribute incentives across a broader band of teachers, and not necessarily on a perma-nent basis. Incentives have even been held back and paid out in 'bonus' form at the end of a financial year to those teachers deemed to have merited such an *ex-gratia* payment. Governors of schools where such strategies are suggested should relate their decisions to clear targets for teachers; clear understanding by all involved as to how the system works; and the knowledge that some teachers will inevitably describe them as a 'performance-related' scheme. Governors will discover that this is a very sensitive area, where clear guidelines and criteria should be agreed in advance with the whole staff. Governors and staff will work together far more effectively in an atmosphere of open partnership and with clear lines of communication.

Enhancement of salaries basically applies to heads and deputies. Depending upon the size of the school, every head and deputy is paid at an indicative (DES) point on a national scale. At present this consists of 51 salary points. The heads and deputies are placed at a point in one of six groups (four for special schools) which indicates their prospective salary. These groupings are:

Size of school	Headteachers	Deputies
Group 1	Point 3–15	Point 1–8
Group 2 1(S)	Point 8–22	Point 2–10
Group 3 2(S)	Point 15–29	Point 4–13
Group 4 3(S)	Point 23–37	Point 8–20
Group 5 4(S)	Point 31–44	Point 15–26
Group 6	Point 38–51	Point 22–34
S = special school		

Let us suppose that the headteacher of a Group 2 school (dependent upon the size of his/her school and his/her experience) is at an indicative point 12. The deputy is on point 5. The governing body could, at its discretion, either on request or on its own initiative consider enhancing the head's and/or deputy's salary. This could mean moving them one or more points up the group scale (at present each point move would cost the school about £400). They cannot be moved upwards out of their group unless the governors make a specific request to the appropriate authority.

What criteria should governors use when considering enhancement of heads' and deputies' salaries

The national criteria suggested by the DFE are:

- the responsibilities of the post;
- the social, economic and cultural background of the pupils attending the school;
- whether the post is difficult to fill; and
- sustained overall performance by the headteacher or deputy

headteacher which appreciably exceeds that normally expected from the holders of such posts.

However, governing bodies may use criteria decided by themselves which should include the following considerations:

- Is the salary adequate having regard to the duties, responsibilities or performance of the head or deputy or the circumstances of the school? If not, what should be an appropriate higher salary?
- Can the school budget afford such an enhancement, both now and in the future?

Governors may like to ponder on ideas such as the setting of performance targets and success criteria, with the result that heads/deputies could be paid a 'bonus' at the end of the financial year instead of an enhancement.

The whole question of enhancement has so far proved extremely confused and has often produced friction between senior management and governors. This situation is compounded when comparisons are made with other heads/deputies in similar schools who have received enhancements. Governors need to concentrate on their own school; on its particular characteristics, and on the overall performance of the people involved. It should be pointed out that some heads and governors are philosophically opposed to enhancement on the grounds that their salary, as indicated, is adequate and that any surpluses should benefit the school directly. Governors need to set clear guidelines and reach an open agreement with their headteacher and deputy on enhancement policy.

Two final points:

- governors cannot place heads/deputies *below* their indicative point, and
- governors may advertise each of these posts when there is a vacancy at whatever point on the salary scale (within the school grouping) they wish. They may wish to consider the sort of people they wish to attract to the job when deciding the point at which it may be advertised. Equally they may wish to be non-committal on the salary and negotiate with their favoured candidate(s).

Budgeting teachers' salaries

The Government has directed that a new salary structure be used from September 1st 1993. It is intended that the new structure will:

- ensure that pay incentives raise and sustain motivation;
- improve recruitment and retention by showing clear pay progression prospects; and
- achieve a closer relationship between performance and pay.

Governors will have to consider the teaching experience of teachers; their training qualifications; any extra responsibilities they may have in the school; and their classroom and job performance. This is a completely new situation for governors which will clearly be a very sensitive issue, where a clearly recognised and workable structure within the school will be necessary. The needs of the school and what it can afford will once more be paramount. Careful preparation and decision-making based on clear evidence will be vital for the successful implementation of this major governor responsibility.

Budgeting the costs of supply teachers

Depending upon local circumstances, schools will probably be paying between £100–£120 per day for a supply teacher plus, possibly, a claim for travel (£5–£10). Supply teachers are used by schools to cover for absence of permanent staff away for reasons of sickness, attendance at courses, etc. Schools sometimes plan to use supply teachers on a regular part-time basis. This may be to cover for a regular absence of a member of staff, perhaps for administrative reasons, or because the supply teacher offers expertise in a specific curriculum area which the school has identified as a need.

In general, schools are advised to plan a supply budget on a 'worst-case' scenario; in other words, to allow a figure which will cover perhaps a lengthy individual staff illness. Some LEAs will take responsibility for payment of supply teachers over a certain formula threshold for each school. This may entail the school taking out an insurance for each member of staff. In this way the school could be covered for all eventualities. Often the school will be pleasantly surprised by its low level of supply claim during the year and may have a reasonable surplus to carry forward to the next financial year. There are commercial schemes of supply insurance which should be studied very carefully in view of certain exclusions. Governors should treat this area of supply staff with considerable caution and are advised to work on the maxim that it is better to be safe than sorry.

Budgeting for non-teaching staff

This covers administrative and/or secretarial staff, technicians and non-teaching assistants in classrooms. Schools, increasingly, are adopting a 'creative' approach to the use of 'non-teachers'. As their salary structure is somewhat below that of teaching staff, some schools are finding it more appropriate to employ 'non-teachers' as a consistent reinforcement to teaching staff. By the judicious use of 'non-teachers' under the direct management of teachers, schools are actually cutting down on their salary costs without lowering the standard of education offered to the children.

This strategy can be very successful but requires careful management and monitoring. It is a sensitive area, and should not be looked upon simply as a way to save money by cutting down on teachers' salaries. There has also been a long-standing tendency by schools to take advantage of the goodwill of secretaries/administrators who consistently work longer hours, and use far greater skills, than they are paid for. Larger schools have started employing bursars to oversee mainly the financial aspects of schools. Again, governors need to consider carefully the needs of the school, the needs of the job which they are offering and finally whether the budget can afford the salary on a medium/long-term basis. Governors may also consider whether a bonus to salary could be offered at the end of the financial year to every 'non-teacher' who has given conspicuous service to the school.

Budgeting for midday supervision and caretaking

These are not consistent budget areas nationally and much depends on local conditions and arrangements. Governors should be aware of the conditions in their school and when involved in financial decision-making in either of these aspects must always consider first – 'What are the needs of the school?' Corner-cutting is not advised.

B. SUPPLIES AND SERVICES

This is the second major area of school spending and covers items such as books, educational equipment and materials, office expenses, cleaning materials, furniture, examination fees, etc. Every authority or school will probably have variations on such a list, but basically it is all about the material resources needed to enhance the children's education and the resources needed by staff to run the school. This, of course, will require careful planning and governors should see a strong relationship here between the school plan and its use of finance.

Money should be allocated on a systematic basis to identified areas of need, and not apportioned necessarily on an 'equal share' basis. It is simply not possible to achieve the 'ideal' school situation in one year; options will need to be prioritised on the basis of clear planning and need. In that way the budget target for the school can be met, and, if medium-term planning (2–3 years) is also taking place, then other priorities will be identified in the following years. Schools will probably be spending 5–6 per cent of their budget on supplies and services. A significantly greater or lesser percentage should have a clear explanation.

C. PREMISES MAINTENANCE, ENERGY, WATER

These concern the fabric of the building where education is taking place. Governors often feel they have particular knowledge to offer the school here because of their own commercial, industrial or professional knowledge. Schools are allocated a sum for maintenance based upon variable factors determined by the authorities. Governors should at all times consider their main guideline to be the safety of the children. If buildings or grounds are inadequately maintained, for whatever reason, then the governors are responsible and, in the case of damage or accident, must hope that they have not been negligent.

The Management of Health and Safety at Work Regulations (1992) came into force on 1st January 1993. They require employers to make assessments of workplace risks to the safety of employees and others who may be affected (for example children) in the case of schools. Competent persons should be appointed to assist in the implementation of the necessary health and safety provisions. The competent person should have received sufficient training, knowledge and experience to undertake these tasks. In other words, the governors would be wise to gain the advice of an expert on health and safety, probably annually, on the maintenance needs of the school, which may not always be obvious to the inexperienced eye. This again is an area where it would be inadvisable to cut corners; governors should be vigilant when considering tenders, and 'lowest price' may not always be the most appropriate choice. Maintenance of buildings will become a more pressing problem for schools without consistent monitoring.

Monitoring is also needed when planning spending on energy and water. Previous years' consumption should be examined and used as comparisons. Planning should indicate times of the year and probable cost of most energy bills. A policy of simple energy conservation could be encouraged throughout the school – closing doors, switching off

12

lights, etc. Common sense is needed, though, since dropping the temperature of the school to an uncomfortable level is not an appropriate method of efficient budgeting. Regular monitoring of consumption will soon indicate inconsistencies which can be investigated. Percentage expenditure will vary between schools due to their differing construction and age.

Finally, governors should be aware that when their school receives an OFSTED inspection in future it will be the duty of the inspectors to:

> include clear reference to any aspect of the school, whether of provision or practice, which in their judgement constitutes a threat to health or safety and any breaches of the law.

(OFSTED – Framework for Inspection)

5. Surpluses and other income

Governors should, by now, have a reasonable knowledge as to the school budget – where it comes from – why it is at the level it is – and the areas of expenditure which it covers. There are two further financial aspects to consider.

Firstly, 'contingency', defined as the surplus carried forward, underspent in a previous year, or the planned underspend for the current year. This is a combination of an 'emergency' fund and a planned future spending fund, and governors should be aware of its existence and the reasons for it.

Secondly, income from other sources. This could take a variety of forms – lettings of all or part of the school premises – donations – sponsorship etc. Schools have numerous ways of supplementing their budget, and not all of them can be planned very far in advance, or the results forecast. However, it would be useful for governors to ascertain an approximate figure if possible, so that it may be taken into account for future planning. Governors may well decide to allocate this addition to a specific resource or project in school.

6. Optional activities for governors: typical budget issues

At this point, governors may like to examine a few issues which could arise in the management of the school budget. The school management structure will dictate how the problems are approached, but governors should bear in mind their overall financial duties. How might you approach these situations?

ISSUE 1 – The governors' finance sub-committee reports a budget surplus projection of £25,000 for the current financial year. What information would you need in determining the use or otherwise of this surplus? Has your governing body any strategies for deciding future budget priorities for the school?

ISSUE 2 – The head indicates that at the next governors meeting he will be requesting a rise of 3 points on the national salary scale for himself. How would you react to this? What questions do you think you might ask of him? Are there any criteria relating specifically to your school which you might like to apply?

ISSUE 3 – The school is offered up to £7,500 for any project it cares to name, so long as it can match equally the donation (50/50 basis). No allowance for this has been made in the budget, and the donation can only be made in this financial year. How would you set about resolving this issue? What are the implications of private fund-raising? What might be your reasons for turning down the offer?

ISSUE 4 – At a finance sub-committee meeting the head indicates that about £4,000 is available owing to underspending on supply. Priorities have been identified such as purchasing more modern computers; replacing obsolete reference library books; help for the more able children, and the need for more expertise in the teaching of music. What criteria would you suggest for making decisions based upon this information?

ISSUE 5 – An inspection of the school buildings indicates badly peeling paintwork on doors and windows; cracks in windows of two classrooms; uneven paving slabs in parts of the playground; poor door closure mechanism on several doors; worn carpet areas in three classrooms; several dripping hot water taps and a leaking PE shed roof. Estimates from two local builders average £5,500 for all the work. The budget plan for the year has allocated £3,500 for maintenance. How would you deal with this issue?

7. Summary

These are typical examples of situations faced in schools under LMS. Not all governors will be involved in taking decisions on such financial matters. However, it is as well that they know of the decisions and the ways in which they are reached. The governors have wide financial powers under the Education Reform Act and should be well aware of these responsibilities. Governors may like to ask themselves the question – 'Will I have any personal financial liability as a consequence of my duties?' The simple answer is that by law the governors will bear no financial liability *if they act in good faith*. When governors are acting under powers delegated to them by the LEA, they must take the same amount of care in discharging their responsibilities òn behalf of the LEA as they would take in their own affairs. However, governors should be aware that they could incur personal liability if they enter into agreements or carry out actions on behalf of the school which are *ultra vires*, i.e. outside the scope of their capacity under the articles of government of the school, or otherwise involve misfeasance; in other words they must work within their defined areas of responsibility. If governors have any worries about their personal liability, they will be reassured by the fact that wide-ranging insurance for personal liability is available for an annual premium of approximately £30.

The main purpose of a school is to deliver high-quality education to its pupils. Finance is only a part of the essential overall planning process. If governors are able to help with the school plan; advise on the consequent setting of the budget; join in prioritising and decision-making processes; effectively monitor the budget and communicate regularly with each other and the school management, then they will gain great satisfaction in the successful implementation of their financial responsibilities.

Further reading

DES Circulars 7/88 and 7/91.
LMS Initiative Manual, *A Practical Guide* (CIPFA).
Management within Primary Schools, The Audit Commission.
Budget Management Pack – Management Development Services (NAHT), 141 High Street, Old Portsmouth PO1 2HY.
OFSTED 1, *Framework for Inspection of Schools*, DES.
Governor Insurance, Jardines Educational Service (with help line).

The author acknowledges the contribution to this chapter of Mr Rodney Braithwaite, Headteacher, Flyford Flavell First School, Worcester.

CHAPTER 2
Appointing Staff

Introduction

A school's most valuable resource is its staff – teaching and non-teaching. Perhaps therefore the most important decisions which governing bodies have to make are those which concern the recruitment and selection of staff. Not only is it important to find the 'right' person, but also a mistake can be expensive in another way. A teacher appointed at £15,000 will cost almost ten times as much over a period of five years when employers' National Insurance and salary increases are taken into account.

Governors need, therefore, to make the right decision for the good of the school. This chapter is designed to take you through the stages of recruitment and selection, suggesting ways in which you might develop an effective process in your school. Although the advice refers specifically to teaching staff, the principles apply to non-teaching staff also.

STAGE 1 Identify the requirements of the job vacancy to be filled

Future staffing needs of a school should be clear from the school development plan, with its projection over at least three years, based on the aims of the school.

The job vacancy can be defined on the basis of a comprehensive staffing audit of present and future requirements. This should include such details as:

- the optimum number of staff required to run the school and to deliver the full curriculum;
- the ages and qualifications of staff in post;
- patterns of promotion within the school and the level and frequency of staff promotions out of the school;

- school numbers and predictions of growth, which will affect the budget.

STAGE 2 The job description and the job specification

A job description should be **SMART** if suitable candidates are to be encouraged to apply. It should be:

Specific – what exactly is required in terms of subjects to be taught, particularly skills and knowledge required, particular responsibilities etc?

Manageable – does the post and the salary offered fit into the planned development of the school?

Achievable – are you likely to find a suitable applicant for the post when you consider the requirements and the salary?

Realistic – in relation to predictions of the growth of the school and other information, are you able to offer a full-time permanent post or should you be looking at the possibilities of temporary appointments?

Time-lined – when is it necessary for the successful candidate to take up the post? This will help you to plan the recruitment and selection process.

The job specification is often combined with the job description. It should include:

- the knowledge, skills and personal qualities required;
- the qualifications and experience required;
- any special requirements, e.g. experience of running SIMS networks.

Drafting an effective job description

It is important to establish responsibilities for drawing up a job description and for advertising a post. Governors of voluntary-aided schools have different responsibilities from those of maintained schools who manage their own budget. The type of vacancy will also determine responsibilities.

The following questions may be helpful in formulating an appropriate job description:

- What is the title of the post?
- What is the status of the post-holder?
- Where in the context of the existing structure of the school does the post fit?
- To whom is the post-holder responsible?
- For what is the post-holder responsible?
- For whom is the post-holder responsible?
- To whom does the post-holder relate?
- What are the general duties of the post-holder?
- What are the specific duties of the post-holder?
- How is the performance of the post-holder to be monitored and by what criteria?
- What provisions are to be made for future development of the job description?

ACTIVITY 2
In your school what are the arrangements for appointing a headteacher or a deputy?
Who draws up the job description?
Who advertises the post?
Where will it be advertised?
What are the arrangements for appointments to other posts?

The job description is sent out to those who respond to the job advertisement, with other particulars. Advertising space costs money but it attracts attention and can state that application forms and detailed information are available on request.

Other particulars

In addition to the job description and the application form candidates need further information about the school. This includes:

- a description of the school – its location and catchment area, age range, number on roll, size and organisation of staff, structure of teaching groups, teaching methods and facilities;
- a statement of the school aims;
- a statement of the aims of the relevant department;

- a date for short-listing;
- the date for interview;
- the selection criteria;
- the organisation of the interview;
- the method of notifying candidates of success or otherwise;
- the opportunity for and arrangements for a debriefing;
- an invitation to visit the school.

It is becoming common practice for headteachers to visit schools in which the candidates teach and to observe them in the classroom. If this is school policy, then details of how it could be arranged should be included.

It is important to remember that at all stages of the recruitment and selection process, governors must adhere to employment regulations, particularly those relating to equal opportunities. This applies to the job description and other supporting information as well as the conduct of the interview. Phrases such as 'applications from men are especially welcome' can be legal if the gender of the successful applicant is a genuine occupational qualification. Governing bodies also have a legal responsibility to prevent unlawful discrimination on grounds of marital status, colour, race, or nationality.

STAGE 3 Identifying selection criteria

Criteria for selection need to be carefully defined. They provide a screening procedure or checklist which helps you to make a decision about the suitability of the candidates. The figure opposite shows a possible format for drawing up selection criteria.

ACTIVITY 3
The first two sections of criteria for the post of a deputy head are completed for you. Complete the remainder, thinking possibly of the appointment of a deputy head in your own school.

POST TITLE	Deputy head		
CRITERIA	Essential	Desirable	Notes
PHYSICAL	Health		
QUALIFICATIONS	Teaching qualification Degree	Higher degree Knowledge of IT management systems	
EXPERIENCE	Successful experience in a post of responsibility. Successful teaching experience in similar school		
INSERVICE TRAINING			
SPECIAL APTITUDES	Knowledge of National Curriculum		
DISPOSITION	Good team member		
SKILLS	Good communication skills		

STAGE 4 Short-listing

Information for short-listing candidates for interview comes chiefly from candidates' application forms.

ACTIVITY 4
How effective is the design of your application form? Is it clear for all concerned? Does it invite the candidate to provide the information you need? Is it designed to enable you to screen out unsuitable candidates? Does it indicate areas for the preparation of questions to be asked at interview?

When application forms seem to give little opportunity for the candidate to make clear his/her views and philosophies, it is useful to ask for additional information, whether on a specific area relating to the post or as an invitation to write, in a limited number of words, about educational aims.

Information on candidates can also come from references. These are confidential documents written by people named by candidates as willing to support their application. A request for a reference should be accompanied by a copy of the job description and the further particulars which have been sent out to candidates.

The value of references is sometimes questioned. They are written in the context of another school and reflect opinions and prejudices of the referee. Some councils, in line with their equal opportunities employment policy, advise taking up references on successful candidates only, to ensure that selection panels are not influenced by the views of others when making a decision. It is also possible to take up references on short-listed candidates only.

Whichever method is adopted, the time required for references to be returned must be fitted into the planned recruitment and selection process. Arrangements for calling for references should be explained to candidates in the further particulars about the posts which are sent to them.

STAGE 5 Preparation for the selection interview

In many schools the selection of staff includes more than an interview before a selection panel. Candidates may be encouraged to show their expertise in a variety of ways:

- by running a meeting;
- by making a presentation;
- by means of a problem-solving exercise;
- by means of psychometric tests.

An extended interview, over two days, will enable candidates to meet and to be involved in discussions with key teachers with whom they will be working, with members of the local Inspectorate and with governors. Such a variety of perspectives should help governors to decide who is the best candidate for their school.

The objective of a selection interview is straightforward – to select the best person available for the job. There is, however, a need for the school to give an equally good impression to the outside world. To a certain extent, the interview is a public relations exercise. Those successful and those not successful all leave with an impression of the organisation. That impression will be derived largely from the interviewing panel.

A successful selection interview requires careful preparation and planning if it is to run smoothly. This need not take hours, just good, common-sense planning. However many candidates there are for a job, it will entail only one preparation exercise. In preparation for the formal interview, those involved should meet to agree:

- how the interview should be conducted;
- what the job involves;

- what sort of person could fulfil it;
- a list of areas needing to be covered;
- what each member of the panel will ask;
- the order of the questioning.

Questions should be short and clear if you are to receive an adequate response. They should be open-ended, beginning with 'how' or 'why' or 'when', or any form which encourages the candidate to talk and which gives them the opportunity to show themselves to advantage.

Closed questions generally result in a 'yes' or 'no' response and are appropriate when factual information is required.

Governing bodies, because of their composition, possess a range of skills which will prove invaluable in the interviewing context. You may, however, find the following checklist helpful:

- ask open questions to get the conversation underway and to encourage the interviewee to talk;
- ensure that you get answers to the questions you have posed by using specific questions;
- start with a relatively straightforward question especially if the candidate seems shy or nervous;
- prepare any hypothetical questions you may wish to use in advance. These are a useful means of inviting candidates to describe how they would think through and approach a problem;
- watch and listen carefully to both what is said and how it is said;
- make brief notes to remind you of points made or inconsistencies which may need further probing. You may wish to ask interviewees at the outset if they mind you taking notes.

STAGE 6 Conducting a successful interview

An interview is a stressful time for both candidates and interviewers. The selection panel is anxious to select the most suitable candidate for its school. Candidates are anxious to show themselves at their best.

Certain courtesies help to create a climate which is businesslike and friendly. Included among these should be:

- the information which is sent to candidates should help them to prepare for the interview;
- confirmation of the date, time, form and place of interview should be sent in writing to the candidate;

- candidates should be met and given hospitality prior to the interview;
- at the beginning of the formal interview candidates should be greeted and introduced to the panel members;
- all members of the panel should have a copy of the candidates' application forms, the selection criteria and questions which they have undertaken to ask;
- reference should be made to the application form to show that it has been read;
- a clock which is visible to the panel will enable them to keep track of the time without looking repeatedly at their watches;
- the candidates should be offered the chance of asking questions if they wish;
- it should be made quite clear when the interview has ended.

Candidates should leave the interview feeling that they have had every opportunity to present themselves as favourably as possible.

STAGE 7 Making the decision

Careful preparation and attention to the recruitment and selection process can minimise the possibility of choosing the 'wrong' person.
A panel may fail to make the correct selection by:

- picking the wrong candidate i.e. failing to expose weaknesses because of poorly prepared questioning;
- missing the right candidate i.e. failing to provide the opportunities for candidates to express their experience, skills and qualities.

Be on the look-out for inconsistencies, uncertainties, omissions. Listen to the answers to other questions, as well as to your own. Do not be fooled by the extrovert or mistake quietness for reserve.
Above all, use the selection criteria as the point of reference, making notes against each one as the interview progresses. This will help you to focus and to listen.

STAGE 8 After selection

A new member of staff will need support from teaching colleagues but do not underestimate the support which the staff as a whole need from a good working relationship with the governing body. The indicators of such a relationship are:

- an active interest in what the staff contribute to the school;
- an appreciation of their contributions;
- a concern for staff development;
- a good working environment;
- an understanding of the stresses experienced by teachers;
- a fair hearing of disputes.

ACTIVITY 5
- do you know the names of all the staff?
- can you put names to faces?
- do you know what each one does?
- what opportunities does the school provide for staff development?

The quality of your recruitment and selection procedures reflects your relationship with the staff. Concern to select the right person and knowledge as to which candidate is the right person come from a good working relationship between governors and staff.

Further advice and reading

Equal Opportunities Commission – Overseas House, Quay Street, Manchester M3 3HN.

Grant-maintained School Centre, Wesley Court, 4a Priory Road, High Wycombe HP13 6SE.

Effective Staff Selection in Schools, Colin Hume, Action for Governors' Information and Training, Longman.

Picking the team; how to choose the right staff for your school, Video Arts, or Local Authority Governor Training Groups.

The author acknowledges the contribution to this chapter of Mrs Janet Fielding, Advisory Teacher, Hereford and Worcester LEA.

CHAPTER 3
Behaviour Management

Introduction

This chapter aims to help governors to fulfil their responsibilities in relation to behaviour management in school. These responsibilities are set down in statute in the articles of Government. In addition, there are recommendations for good practice in The Elton Committee report entitled *Discipline in Schools: Report of the Committee of Inquiry*, published by HMSO in March 1989. Generally, governors' responsibilities fall in three areas:

- contributing to the development of a whole-school behaviour policy;
- the appointment of staff;
- the exclusion procedures for an individual pupil.

In exercising their responsibilities in this area, governors may find it helpful to refer to the following summary of the findings of the Elton Committee which set out to consider what action could be taken by Government, LEAs, governors, headteachers, teachers and parents to 'secure the orderly atmosphere necessary in schools for effective teaching and learning to take place'. The report was compiled from evidence provided by individual submissions, interviews with 100 teachers and questionnaires sent to 3,500 teachers.

What kind of discipline problem is there in schools?

The results of the Elton Committee Survey are as follows:

(a) How serious do you think the problem of discipline is in your school?

In only one in twenty primary schools did teachers think the problem was verging on the 'serious'. Two out of three teachers thought the problems were 'not at all serious' or 'no problem at all'. Four out of ten primary teachers said they had no difficult pupils in their classes.

One in six secondary school teachers thought the problems of discipline were 'serious'. The majority (53 per cent) thought they were 'not very serious' but only 4 per cent thought there was 'no problem at all'. Two out of ten secondary teachers said that they had no difficult pupils in their classes.

(b) What types of pupil behaviour do you have to deal with over the course of a week?

Percentage of primary teachers	Problems in lessons (at least once a week)
97%	talking out of turn
90%	hindering other pupils
85%	making unnecessary noise
74%	physical aggression to other pupils
73%	getting out of seat without permission
67%	calculated idleness
60%	general rowdiness
55%	verbal abuse to other pupils
50%	persistently infringing class rules
16%	physical destructiveness
7%	verbal abuse to teachers
2%	physical aggression to teacher

Secondary teachers	
97%	talking out of turn
87%	calculated idleness
86%	hindering other pupils
82%	being late
77%	making unnecessary noise
68%	persistently infringing rules
62%	getting out of seat
62%	verbal abuse of other pupils
42%	physical aggression to other pupils
15%	verbal abuse of teachers
2%	physical aggression towards teachers

26

(c) How do you and your school try to deal with difficult pupils and difficult classes?

Percentage of primary teachers	Strategies
80%	reasoning with pupils, class discussions
71%	removing privileges
61%	extra work
33%	keeping pupils in

Secondary teachers

92%	reasoning with pupils in class
89%	reasoning with pupils out of class
76%	extra work
71%	deliberate ignoring
67%	detention
66%	class discussion
61%	asking pupils to withdraw from class
50%	referral to another teacher
44%	removal of privileges
27%	sending to senior member of staff
9%	requesting suspension

(d) What action do you think might best be taken to help with the problems of discipline in your school?

Percentage of primary and secondary teachers	
57%	establishing smaller classes
30%	tougher sanctions
34%	more opportunities for counselling
32%	more parental involvement

In summary the Elton Committee concluded that the vast majority of teachers have to deal with minor disruptions on a regular basis and that their cumulative effort 'contributes to a sense of stress and growing frustration'.

ACTIVITY 1 Sharing concerns about behaviour

Consider the following questions and discuss your responses as they apply to your own particular school. Compare your responses with the results of the survey.

    (a) How serious do you think the problem of discipline is in your school?
    (b) What sort of behaviour problems are there?
    (c) How do staff try to deal with difficult pupils and difficult classes?
    (d) What action do you think might best be taken to help with the problems of discipline in your school?

What contribution can governors make to a whole-school behaviour policy?

The Elton Committee recommended that 'headteachers and teachers should, in consultation with their governors, develop whole-school behaviour policies which are clearly understood by pupils, parents and other school staff'. The committee suggested that governors can and should make a positive contribution to whole-school approaches to pupils' behaviour. Such a contribution could include:

1. A written statement of general principles for the school behaviour policy

Governors have the powers to draw up a written statement of general principles to guide the headteacher. The head has to act in accordance with this statement. The head is responsible for putting any general principles set up by the governors into practice and for dealing with individual cases.

When governors choose to draw up a written statement of general principles for a school's behaviour policy, they should take account of the principles of good practice in the Elton report. Successful policies are likely to have the following characteristics:

Values

The policy should be based on a set of clear and defensible principles or values. These principles should be consistent with the school's overall aims.

Rules/standards of behaviour

Headteachers should define the aims of the school in relation to standards of behaviour, establish agreement on these standards and ensure these standards are consistently applied.

- the reason behind the rules should be clear
- rules should be derived from the principles underlying their policies
- a few, pertinent rules are more effective than a long list of prohibitions
- rules need to be clearly stated and, as far as possible, unambiguous
- rules should be realistic and fair
- as far as possible, rules should be phrased positively
- if possible, pupils, parents and governors should be involved in the formulation of rules.

Rewards and sanctions

For rules to be effective they need to be built into a system of sanctions for breaking them and rewards for keeping them. The Elton Committee recommended that 'schools should strike a healthy balance between rewards and punishments and that both should be clearly specified'. They emphasised that 'schools which put too much faith in punishment to deter bad behaviours are likely to be disappointed'. 'Punitive regimes seem to be associated with worse rather than better standards of behaviour.' However, the Committee went on to say, 'this does not mean that punishments are not necessary'. The Committee recommended that 'pupils should learn from experience to expect fair and consistently applied punishments for bad behaviour which make the distinction between serious and minor offences apparent'. There may need to be flexibility in the use of punishments to take account of individual circumstances. Headteachers and teachers should avoid the punishment of whole groups and punishments which humiliate.

Involvement of staff

The Elton Committee recognised the importance of all staff being involved in the school's behaviour policy and taking responsibility for standards of behaviour throughout the school.

Involvement of parents

The Elton Committee emphasised the importance of parental involvement in the school's behaviour policy. Recommendations include informal contact with parents, parental help in class and at home, early involvement of parents over particular children with behaviour problems, good channels of communication and ensuring parents are aware of the school's behaviour policy.

ACTIVITY 2 Statement of principles for a behaviour policy

Using the following questions as a guide, produce a written statement of general principles for a school behaviour policy.

(a) What are your aims in relation to behaviour in the school? How would you like people to treat each other in school?

(b) What are your attitudes on rewards and punishment?

(c) What is your view on the link between curriculum/teaching methods and behaviour?

(d) What do you think should be involved in the development of a school's behaviour policy?

(e) How can teachers be supported in dealing with behaviour problems?

---

2. Monitoring standards of behaviour

Behaviour policies need to be monitored and evaluated. The Elton Committee recommended that governors should obtain regular reports on the standards of behaviour in their schools from headteachers. The committee also recommended that governors' annual reports should contain a section on the standards of behaviour and attendance at the school.

ACTIVITY 3 Example behaviour policy

Consider the example behaviour policy on pages 37–42 and offer comments in relation to the following:

(a) what you like about the example policy;

(b) what improvement suggestions you have.

How can governors ensure that they appoint staff who are skilled in managing pupils' behaviour?

Clearly, the appointment of staff who are well-skilled in managing pupils is essential if the school's behaviour policy is to work in practice. The Elton Committee emphasised the important role which governors play in appointing staff and the need for them to ensure that they look for the personal qualities required for managing a school or classroom effectively:

> We recommend that in appointing Headteachers governors should take care to

select only those candidates who have the leadership and management qualities necessary for establishing whole school behaviour policies.

In appointing other staff, governors should take care to select candidates temperamentally suited to staff team work and mutual support and able to form relationships with pupils based on mutual respect.

ACTIVITY 4 Appointment of staff

In a small group, address the questions listed below:

(a) In your view, what personal qualities are required for managing a class effectively?
(b) What questions would you ask to find out if the applicant had these qualities?

What should schools do to help children with behaviour difficulties?

Governors' responsibilities in relation to individual pupils are 'at the end of the line' when a child has been excluded from school as a result of behaviour problems. Decisions about the day-to-day management of a particular pupil or of pupils in general are the responsibility of the headteacher and his/her teaching staff, and are not the province of the governing body. However, it is useful for governors to be aware of the steps which schools should go through, and the support which is available to schools, prior to any consideration of the use of exclusion procedures for a child with behavioural problems.

Evidence suggests that certain pupils are more likely to present behaviour or attendance problems than others. Boys are four times more likely to be involved in exclusion than girls. They are more likely to be rated as of below average ability and to have a history of low achievement at school. These 'risk profiles' must be treated with caution. They can result in self-fulfilling prophecy. However, 'risk profiles' can sharpen teachers' awareness of potential problems so that there are possibilities for preventative measures before patterns are set.

A step-by-step approach

1. The classteacher

The first source of help for an individual pupil experiencing behaviour difficulties is the pupil's classteacher. The first step will be to investigate possible causes of the problem – for example, whether the work is too difficult, whether the pupil is having problems at home, whether there is something worrying the pupil. Results of investigations will influence the approaches and strategies used by the teacher, such as giving the pupil extra attention for good behaviour or extra responsibilities to develop self-esteem. In most cases the help of a skilled classteacher will be sufficient to overcome the pupil's difficulties. However, for some pupils, if difficulties persist, it is time to involve the parents.

2. Parental involvement

Parental involvement should be as early as possible. This allows parents to become involved in helping the school to tackle problems before they have become severe. The aim of parental involvement should be to discuss how parents and school can work together to help the pupil overcome the difficulties. For most pupils this may be sufficient to overcome their difficulties. However, for some pupils a more thorough investigation involving other memebers of staff in school is needed.

3. Involvement of other staff in school

The next step is for advice and support to be sought from other staff in the school – for example colleagues, special needs coordinator, headteacher. It may be that practical support is needed; perhaps sending the child to another teacher for 'time out' when problems arise. It may be that assessment of learning difficulties by the special needs coordinator is required. It may be that staff need to work together to adopt a consistent approach to the pupil's difficulties. In most cases this is sufficient to overcome difficulties. However, where difficulties persist, this is the time to involve outside agencies for support.

4. Support services

A number of different support services are available to help schools tackle individual behaviour problems. These services include Educational Psychology, Learning Support, Child Guidance, Social Services, Education Welfare. These services work in different ways to help pupils. For most, the involvement of one or more of these services, working in conjunction with the school and family, will be sufficient to overcome the difficulties. However, there are a small number of pupils whose difficulties persist. For these pupils there is a choice, depending on the circumstances.

5a. Referral for formal assessment (1981 Act)

This is necessary if the pupil is thought to have long-term emotional and behavioural difficulties which require the education authority to make special educational provision. Most LEAs have some provision for pupils with severe behaviour difficulties – either in special schools or off-site units.

5b. Exclusion

This can be for a fixed or indefinite period of time and may result in a range of options including reinstatement, change of school or teaching in a small group out of school.

ACTIVITY 5 Case studies

Below are a number of possible situations which you might have to deal with as a governor. In small groups, discuss your responses to the issues raised. Bear in mind the distinction between your responsibilities as a governor and the responsibilities of the headteacher. You may wish to refer to the 'comments on case studies' after your deliberations.

(a) Several parents have approached you to complain about the behaviour of a pupil. They say that he/she disrupts the lessons for their children and they want something to be done.

(b) A parent has approached you to say that he is worried because his son is being bullied in school. He says that this is not an isolated incident and his son is not alone. He feels that there is a real problem of bullying in the school.

(c) The headteacher has expressed concern to you as Chair of governors about one particular pupil in the school. The pupil is persistently in trouble in school, does very little work and generally seems to be getting very little out of school. The headteacher simply wants to keep you informed at this stage in case the situation deteriorates further and he has to consider exclusion.

(d) You are concerned about what you consider to be the relatively high number of exclusions in the school where you are a governor. You wonder if there might be more constructive ways of dealing with the problem of discipline.

(e) The headteacher expresses concern to you as Chair of governors about a member of staff who is having difficulty managing his/her class.

Comments on case studies

(a) Governors do not have a role, prior to exclusion, in relation to the behaviour of individual pupils in school. However, governors should always be ready to pass on information and concerns from parents to the proper person to deal with such matters; in this case this is the headteacher. In this situation one of the most useful functions of a school governor would be to encourage the parents to contact the headteacher themselves to discuss their concerns direct.

(b) Again, school governors do not have a role, prior to exclusion, in relation to individual pupils. However, school governors are responsible for monitoring the effectiveness of the school's behaviour policy and receiving reports on standards of behaviour in general. If there is evidence of a general problem of bullying in school, the governors should ask the headteacher and staff to detail their strategies for tackling this problem.

(c) There is a danger in this situation of the Chair of governors becoming too involved in the individual case, and then not being able to avoid prejudice if the pupil is subsequently excluded by the headteacher.

(d) If governors become concerned about how the school's behaviour policy is working in practice, they can ask for this to be raised for discussion as an agenda item at a governors meeting. The governors may decide that they need to revise their statement of general principles underpinning the behaviour policy.

(e) Governors do not have a direct role to play here, though the headteacher may be looking to you for moral support. The headteachers should be encouraged to investigate ways of seeking support for the teacher, possibly through the involvement of advisory teachers or the school Inspector, or by arranging for the teacher to have advice and support with class management skills. The school appraisal system may provide an opportunity for airing some of the issues with the teacher involved.

What are governors' responsibilities in relation to pupil exclusions?

Who can exclude a pupil?

Only the headteacher has the right to exclude a pupil.

What kind of exclusions are there?

Exclusion is now the term used to indicate that a pupil is barred from attending school. There are three types of exclusion:

(i) fixed – temporary with a specified date of return;
(ii) indefinite – no fixed date of return; may be subject to conditions or further enquiries;
(iii) permanent – expulsion; the pupil cannot return to the school.

What are the grounds for excluding a pupil?

Exclusion should be used as a last resort rather than a normal sanction for bad behaviour.

There are, broadly, two reasons for exclusion:

(i) the pupil's behaviour is unacceptable and could put the safety and welfare of other pupils at risk;

(ii) the school has exhausted all other sanctions and can no longer manage a particular pupil.

What procedures should be followed in exclusions?

Action by the head

When a headteacher excludes a pupil he/she must without delay:

- tell the pupil's parents (if the pupil is under 18) that their child has been excluded and explain why; and
- tell the pupil's parents (if the pupil is under 18) that they have the right to take the matter up with the governing body and the LEA. In the case of a permanent exclusion, there is a right to a formal appeal to the LEA, if the governing body has decided that the pupil should not be reinstated.

If the head decides that an exclusion which was for a fixed or indefinite period should be made permanent, he must tell the parents (if the pupil is under 18). He must also tell the governing body and the LEA of his decision and of the reasons for it.

If a proposed exclusion means that a pupil will have been excluded from the school for more than five days, in total, in any term, or that the pupil will lose the chance of taking a public examination, the head must tell the governing body and the LEA of his decision and the reasons for it.

Action by the governing body and LEA

The governing body has the right to direct the head to reinstate a pupil who has been excluded for a fixed period. The LEA has similar powers, though it must consult the governing body before taking such action.

The governing body has the right to direct the head to reinstate a pupil who has been excluded for an indefinite period, either immediately or on a specified date. The LEA has similar powers, though it must consult the governing body before taking such action. If a pupil has been excluded for an indefinite period, and the governing body has set a reinstatement date which the LEA considers to be too late, the LEA may set an earlier date.

Only the governing body has the right to direct the head to reinstate a pupil who has been excluded permanently (often known as expelled).

The head must comply with directions from the governors and from the LEA. But if there are conflicting directions from the LEA and the governing body about the date of reinstatement, the head must comply with the direction which sets an earlier date for reinstatement. Where the LEA directs the head to reinstate a pupil who has been excluded for an indefinite period the direction ceases to have effect if the head decides to exclude the pupil permanently.

What rights of appeal do parents have?

Parents have the right to make representations to the governors and then the LEA if they oppose the exclusion.

How are governors involved with representations from parents?

If the parents indicate that they wish to make representations, the governors should arrange to consider such representations at their earliest convenience. They may do so as a full body or by delegating this task to a panel of three or five governors which should be formally appointed to deal with such matters on behalf of the governing body. In any informal discussions following an exclusion, governors must take care to avoid prejudicing the formal procedures.

The governors, as a result of considering the representations, may endorse the head's decision to exclude or may reinstate the pupil.

What questions should governors ask in considering whether to uphold exclusion?

What did the pupil do which led to exclusion?
Can this be demonstrated sufficiently?

Does the pupil's behaviour put the safety and welfare of other pupils at risk?
Has the school exhausted all other sanction?
Was this a one-off incident?
Was the behaviour part of an ongoing pattern?
If part of a pattern, has the school done all that it could to deal with the problem. For example:

- clear expectations communicated clearly to the pupil;
- constructive parental involvement;
- involvement of support services
- investigation of causes of misbehaviour;
- evidence of behaviour management strategies tried;
- written records kept.

Are there alternative sanctions or solutions which could be used?

Conclusions

Governors have an important role to play in the area of behaviour management in school. They have responsibilities at a preventative level in helping a school to develop an effective behaviour policy, in monitoring school procedures, monitoring standards of behaviour and, crucially, in the appointment of staff with the personal and professional qualities to make sure that the policy works in practice.

It is the responsibility of the headteacher and the school staff, not the school governors, to take day-to-day decisions about behaviour management strategies and to make decisions about individual pupils. Governors' responsibilities in relation to individual pupils are 'at the end of the line' when a headteacher excludes a pupil from school. Here, governors have a role in hearing parents' representations and making unbiased judgements about whether to uphold pupil exclusions or direct reinstatement of the pupil.

Further reading

School Governors: A Guide to the Law, Department of Education and Science.

Articles of Government

Discipline in Schools, Report of the Committee of Inquiry (The Elton Committee Report), published by HMSO in March 1989.

Example Behaviour Policy

Introduction

This school behaviour policy has been written for teachers, pupils, parents and governors of the school. It has been produced as a result of much discussion between staff, pupils and parents and reflects our current practice in trying to promote high standards of discipline in the school. The document is not set in stone and our aim is to keep our policy under regular review.

If you have any comments on this document we would be pleased to hear them.

Deputy Head
Convenor of Behaviour Policy Group

Beliefs about behaviour

We believe that teaching pupils the skills of self-discipline, cooperation, respect and tolerance are an important part of the curriculum. Without these skills our academic objectives cannot be achieved. Furthermore we believe that these are skills which can be learnt, particularly if we work together with parents to achieve our goals.

We believe that everyone in school has the right to be treated as an individual and with respect. Good relationships are vital to the successful working of a school. We value achievements of every kind – academic and non-academic – and we believe that everyone should have an equal opportunity to achieve their potential. We also believe that young people respond well to high expectations. In our school we expect everyone to work hard and give of their best.

In this school we recognise that problems are normal where young people are learning and testing the boundaries of acceptable behaviour. Our success as a school is tested not by the absence of problems but by the way we deal with them.

Code of conduct

We believe that school rules are most effective if they are phrased as positive expectations for the behaviour of everyone in the school. We prefer to have a few, well chosen rules rather than a long list of prohibitions.

The main rule for all of us in school is that everyone will act with courtesy and consideration to others at all times.

This means that:

1. You treat other people with kindness and respect in the way that you would like them to treat you.
2. In class you make it as easy as possible for everyone to learn. (This means arriving on time and with everything you need for the lesson, beginning and ending the lesson in a courteous and orderly way, listening carefully, following instructions, helping each other and being polite and sensible at all times.)
3. You move gently and quietly about the school. (This means never barging or running or shouting but ready to let people pass, opening doors and helping to carry things.)
4. You always speak politely to everyone (even if you feel in a bad mood) and use a low voice. (Shouting is always discourteous.)
5. You are silent when you are required to be.
6. You keep the school clean and tidy so that it is a welcoming place we can all be proud of. (This means putting litter in the bins, keeping walls and furniture clean and taking care of the displays – particularly of other people's work.)
7. Out of school walking locally or with a school group you should remember that the school's reputation depends on the way you behave.
8. You are neat and tidy in your dress. (Details of the school uniform are listed in the school prospectus.)
9. You should stay within the school bounds unless you have express permission to go out of school and people know where you are. This prevents people from worrying about you unnecessarily.

Rewards

Wherever possible, we aim to be positive in our approach and to notice and reward good behaviour rather than take it for granted. We believe that everyone should have equal access to rewards in our school, not just those who are academically able. Everyone responds to the right kind of reward – the trick is to find out what works for each individual. Staff use a range of rewards to promote good behaviour.

1. Credit marks are awarded to pupils who have produced an excellent piece of work or who have made a consistently good effort with several pieces of work. All pupils, regardless of ability, are able to earn credit marks.
2. Merit certificates are awarded for outstanding achievement. This may be the result of consistently high standards of work or consistent effort. They are generally given out at the end of term.
3. Teachers are encouraged to give written positive comments on pupils' work.
4. Pupils' work is displayed as much as possible.
5. The head, deputy and heads of year are glad to praise pupils' good work or behaviour when it is brought to their attention.
6. Letters are sent home to parents for good behaviour or good work.
7. Pupils' positive achievements (including reference to their behaviour) are noted in their Record of Achievement folders.

Above all, staff take every opportunity to offer praise and encouragement to pupils.

Sanctions

We believe that pupils feel more secure if they know where the boundaries of acceptable behaviour lie and what sanctions will be used if they overstep the mark. We believe that punishment is most effective if it is applied fairly and calmly. The smallest possible punishment that is effective should always be used. Pupils need to know why they are being punished and need to be given an opportunity to make amends. Punishment should be applied in a way that maintains self-respect – punishment should not be used to humiliate and the punishment of whole groups should be avoided.

Within-class sanctions

It is the primary responsibility of staff to discipline pupils themselves rather than sending pupils to more senior members of staff. A range of sanctions are used by staff:

- private reprimand;
- moving seats;
- extra work;
- negative;
- loss of privileges;
- reparation, e.g. litter collection.

Sanctions involving other staff

For pupils who misbehave persistently, or for particularly serious incidents, staff will need to involve other colleagues. Referral, in the first instance, is to the head of year. The school operates a positive report system to monitor a pupil's behaviour.

A range of sanctions may be used by the head of year:

- monitoring behaviour by a report system;
- loss of privileges;
- detention;
- the imposition of additional, but meaningful tasks.

Exclusion from school, for whatever period, is avoided if possible, but may be effective for serious misdemeanours. The ultimate sanction of permanent exclusion is only used in exceptional circumstances, where there has been an extremely serious incident or where there has been a long series of misdemeanours. It is only considered when there is a threat to the provision of efficient education for the majority of children; when their safety or welfare is threatened; where school rules have been persistently flouted; or where physical or verbal violence is offered to staff.

Involving parents

Parents will always be contacted before such sanctions are used. Where detention is used care is taken to ensure that parents are given advance warning.

Involving the education psychologist

If difficulties persist the advice of outside agencies, for example, the educational psychologist will be sought.

School organisation

Staff are committed to the view that many behaviour problems can be prevented, or at least minimised, by good organisational measures. Staff are aware of the need to keep organisational issues under regular review.

Supervision of pupils

Staff are asked to supervise pupils in their movement around the school at change of lesson times. Staff should be in classes to meet their pupils.

Arrangements for break and lunchtime

Pupils have open access to the school during school hours. There are designated areas for activities during wet breaks and lunchtimes.

Environment

The school is well cared for with mainly litter-free grounds and attractive displays of pupils' work inside classrooms and corridors. The caretaker deals with minor repairs as quickly as possible. Pupils are encouraged to share in the responsibility for the school environment, e.g. for designated areas for year groups and pupils' involvement in gardening projects.

Curriculum

Staff are well aware of the link between low academic success and poor standards of behaviour, and work hard to alleviate such problems. Pupils are grouped flexibly most of the time in mixed-ability groups but with some setting, e.g. for English and mathematics. The special needs department offers support wherever possible in mainstream lessons rather than withdrawing pupils. Limited withdrawal for short periods of intensive help with literacy skills is provided for some pupils.

Parents and the community

Parental involvement in all aspects of school life is valued. It is considered to be particularly important in promoting good behaviour.

Staff believe that if parents support the school behaviour policy it is more likely to be effective.

Parents are often to be seen around the school helping in many different activities, e.g. with the library, transporting pupils, or making refreshments for social events. When difficulties arise with individual pupils parents are contacted as soon as possible. This is the responsibility of the head of year in consultation with the form tutor.

Support for teachers

It is recognised that dealing with behaviour difficulties can be very stressful for staff and it is not always easy to ask for help.

Dealing with difficult behaviour is the collective responsibility of all members of staff in the school, not just of the teachers immediately concerned with a particular pupil. Staff are generally very willing to acknowledge when they have difficulties with pupils and to support each other. An excellent school handbook has been produced by a group of staff and this is available for all new teachers in the school. Staff meet informally to share concern and to support each other. They are considering setting up more formal, regular staff meetings with the educational psychologist, to enable the school to respond in the most positive way to difficult behaviour. Some staff are keen to develop their skills in managing small groups within the classroom. The school psychologist has offered to help with this.

The author acknowledges the contribution to this chapter of Ms Gillian Tee, Deputy Principal Educational Psychologist, Hereford and Worcester LEA.

CHAPTER 4
Special Educational Needs

Introduction

What are the legal responsibilities of governors in relation to pupils with special educational needs?

With the implementation of the various Education Acts of the 1980s the duties of governors have increased considerably.

A great deal of attention has been given to matters of finance, teacher appointments and curriculum considerations but, underlying all of these aspects of governors' duties, lies the responsibility for the pupils' educational needs. Within the school population there are children who will have special educational needs. Decisions will need to be made by governing bodies on such issues as resources, staffing, use of support services and the statementing of children.

The 1981 Education Act, based on the Report of the Warnock Committee 1978, provides the framework for the laws relating to special education by:

- adopting a concept of special educational need introduced in the Warnock Report. Formerly children were classified in specified categories of handicap. The Report recommended that the main focus should be on the child himself rather than on his disability. Previously the categories determined the type of provision to be made, whereas the 1981 Act stated that provision should be based on the individual needs of the child, taking into account his strengths as well as his disabilities;
- establishing that a small minority of children with special educational needs – those with the most severe, complex and long-term difficulties – should be formally documented by the local educational authority (LEA), via a statement of special educational need;
- imposing certain duties on LEAs and school governors with regard to making special education provision for:

44

- the statemented pupil (LEA responsibility),
- the large group of children with special educational needs who are not statemented (governor responsibility);
- stating procedures and areas of responsibility for the assessment of special educational needs;
- establishing parents' rights in special education assessment procedures, including the right of appeal.

The 1981 Education Act

The Act states that governors have a duty to:

- *use their best endeavours, in exercising their functions in relation to the school, to secure that the necessary provision is made for any registered pupil who has special educational needs;*

  The teacher is directly responsible for his pupils and he is in a key position to observe their response in the classroom, to recognise the child who is experiencing difficulties in learning, and to try out different approaches to help meet the child's needs. Teachers should be encouraged to keep full records of their pupil's progress and to include information about professional consultations and assessments.

  (Education Act, 1981)

For example if a teacher has identified a difficulty in a pupil's attainments in reading then steps must be taken to identify the cause of the difficulty, leading to attempts to remedy that difficulty.

- *secure that, where the 'responsible person' has been informed by the LEA that a registered pupil has special educational needs, those needs are made known to all those who are likely to teach him.*

  Every school must name a 'responsible person'. This person may be the headteacher, Chair of the governors or another governor, who ensures that all who are likely to teach a pupil are informed that he has special educational needs. For example, all teachers will need to know that a child with visual or auditory difficulties will need to sit in the most advantageous position in the classroom.

- *secure that the teachers in the school are aware of the importance of identifying, and providing for, those registered pupils who have special educational needs (Education Act, 1981, para. 2.5).*

This emphasises the need for a school to have a system for identifying children with special educational needs and a policy on how the school will meet those identified needs. Through a whole-school policy all members of staff can be committed to achieving the same aims.

What is meant by special educational needs?

Special educational needs (SEN) is an umbrella term which is used to cover a wide range of disabilities and learning difficulties. It includes children who:

- are sensorily impaired, e.g. deaf, blind;
- are physically impaired;
- have language difficulties;
- experience social and emotional problems;
- have severe learning difficulties;
- are slow to learn;
- have specific learning difficulties.

The concept of special educational need is one of a continuum of need. The continuum stretches from children giving minor concern and who may need a little extra support, perhaps for a short time, to those children where concerns are major and who may need long-term support in a specialist establishment or resourcing of a specialist nature.

The definition of special educational needs under the 1981 Act excludes a learning difficulty which arises solely because the language of instruction is different from the language of the child's home. Although children from linguistic minorities may experience difficulties, they will not be considered under the provision of the 1981 Act unless they also experience difficulties with learning not arising from problems with the language of instruction. (LEAs have a duty to these children under the provisions of Section 8 of the 1944 Education Act.)

For the purposes of the Act, a pupil may be considered to have special educational needs if he has a learning difficulty which calls for special educational provision to be made for him. A pupil has a 'learning difficulty' if he/she:

- has significantly greater difficulties in learning than the majority of children of the same age;
- has a disability which either prevents or hinders him from making use of educational facilities of a kind generally provided in schools, within the area of the local authority concerned, for children of his age; or
- he is under the age of five and is, or would be if special educational provision were not made for him, likely to fall within one of the above two categories when over that age.

> The extent to which a learning difficulty hinders a child's development depends not only on the nature and severity of that difficulty, but also on the personal resources and attributes of the child, and on the help and support he receives at home and at school. A child's special educational needs are thus related to his abilities as well as his disabilities, and to the nature of his interaction with his environment.
>
> (DES Circular 1/83)

The factors which determine what constitutes special educational provision will vary from area to area depending on the range of provision normally available in the authorities' schools.

'Special educational provision' means:

- in relation to a child who has attained the age of two years, educational provision which is additional to, or otherwise different from, the educational provision made generally for children of his age; and
- in relation to any child under that age, educational provision of any kind.

How many children will have special educational needs?

The Warnock Report (1978), produced by an official Committee of Enquiry set up under Baroness Warnock, estimated that one child in five will have some sort of special educational need at some time in his or her school life, though in practice that incidence might vary greatly from school to school, depending, for example, on the catchment area.

It is likely that out of the 20 per cent of the school population estimated to experience difficulties, about 2 per cent of children will be those causing major concern because their difficulties are so severe and complex they may require extra provision – e.g. in terms of help/support/equipment additional to, or otherwise different from, the resources and facilities generally available in the ordinary school. These are the children who will require statements of special educational need provided by the LEA.

Although about 2 per cent of all school children will be 'statemented', in some authorities the great majority of those children may attend special schools or special units attached to schools. It follows that ordinary schools should not expect 2 per cent of their school population to be statemented. Indeed a school might have no statemented children on roll.

It should be noted that the majority of children with special educational needs as defined in the Act – i.e. those without statements – will continue to be educated within the resources of the ordinary school and will not require the LEA to determine how their needs should best be met. These are the children for whom governors will have particular responsibility.

How are children with special educational needs identified?

The Warnock Report suggested a model for identifying and assessing children's special needs. These procedures should allow for a progressive involvement of teachers and other professionals.

STAGE ONE   The teacher in school becomes concerned that a child is experiencing difficulties and carries out certain actions designed to help the situation. This may include, for example, setting up a particular reading programme, making arrangements for some individual or group work etc.

STAGE TWO   To support further the steps already taken, the classteacher consults the headteacher and the person in school responsible for special educational needs and implements any additional suggestions.

The above actions involve arrangements made within the school and are based on the expertise and resources available. In this way attempts are made to remedy the pupil's difficulties. When a school's arrangements for identifying, assessing and meeting special educational needs are brought into force it is important that the pupil's parents are kept fully informed and are involved as much as possible at every stage.

In most instances these actions will be successful for the majority of pupils because their difficulties will be minor and relatively short term. However, there will be a few children for whom concerns remain. Where the interventions at school do not seem to meet the child's needs, further investigations will be required.

STAGE THREE School staff may choose to seek advice from LEA services such as: educational psychologists, specialist support teachers, speech therapists, advisory teachers. Further actions taken at this stage may include: a behavioural programme, specialist assessment teaching, the use of specific resources etc.

STAGE FOUR A small group of children may continue to give cause for concern and will require a multi-professional assessment referred to as formal assessment.

Following this a statement may be written which identifies the nature of a pupil's special educational needs and which outlines the provision that will be needed in order for that particular pupil's needs to be met. Through this procedure which leads to a formal assessment children with severe or complex learning difficulties are identified.

What is a formal assessment?

The LEA has a responsibility to identify children who have special educational needs which call for the authority – as opposed to the school – to determine the special provision which is necessary.

This duty covers any child who is a registered pupil at an LEA-maintained school, or for whom the LEA has arranged education at a non-maintained or independent school, or who has been brought to their attention as possibly having special educational needs. It extends to all registered pupils between the ages of 2 years up to 19 years if that pupil is still in full-time education.

When a school has made the decision to refer a child for assessment by the LEA they must seek the permission of the pupil's parents.

Upon receiving a request the authority will investigate and decide whether it is appropriate for formal assessment to proceed.

If it is considered appropriate the pupil's parents will receive a formal notice setting out:

- the proposal to assess;
- procedures to be followed in the assessment;
- a named officer who can provide further information;
- parents' rights to make representations about the proposal.

Once the parents have been given the opportunity to comment, advice will be sought from those professionals working with the pupil: doctor, educational psychologist and headteacher, and possibly other relevant agencies and support services. The parents will be asked to contribute to the information.

The formal assessment procedure – which can only be concluded when reports have been provided by a teacher, an educational psychologist and a medical officer as a minimum – may or may not result in the LEA writing a statement of special educational needs.

If a statement is not written, the implication is that the pupil's special needs are such that they can best be met within the normal school situation and do not require any form of additional LEA-funded support, resourcing etc.

What is a statement of special educational needs?

A statement is a legal document which should be completed and signed by an authorised officer of the LEA, after any necessary consultations with other appropriate professionals. Although authorities can design their own statements, they have to follow detailed guidance on its form and content. The form suggested by the Department for Education includes an *Introductory Section* (*Section 1*) and the following main sections:

Section 2 Special educational needs

In making an assessment of a child's special educational needs the LEA must take into consideration any evidence and representations submitted by the child's parents and the advice obtained from professionals.

It is important that assessment should be seen as a partnership between teachers, other professionals and parents in a joint endeavour to discover and understand the nature of the difficulties and needs of individual children.

(DES Circular 1/83)

Assessment is not a single event but a continuous process which should always be closely related to education. It needs to be seen not as an end in itself, but as a means of better understanding the child's difficulties for the purpose of providing a guide to his education and as a basis against which to monitor his progress. In this section of the statement there should be an analysis of the assessment results which includes:

- a description of the child's functioning;
- reference to the child's strengths and weaknesses;
- an outline of the short and longer term objectives (both educational and developmental) the child is expected to achieve.

Section 3 Special educational provision

The LEA has a duty to secure that the pupil is educated in an ordinary school as far as is reasonably practical. In making decisions regarding appropriate provision for a pupil the LEA must take into account:

- the views of the parents;
- the ability of the school to provide the special education required;
- the effect on the education of the other children in the school;
- the efficient use of resources.

The LEA must specify the special educational provision to be made for the child in terms of the facilities and equipment, staffing arrangements, curriculum and other arrangements to be made to meet his special educational needs.

Section 4 Appropriate school or other arrangements

The LEA must describe the type of school they consider appropriate for the child, and name the particular school, if known, or the provision to be made for the child's education if he is to be educated other than at a school.

Section 5 Additional non-educational provision

Details must be provided of any provision which the LEA is satisfied will be made available by any other body (if not provided by the LEA), in addition to the child's special educational provision and as support for his education.

Review of statement

Every statement is subject to review once a year. The review is instigated by the headteacher of the school and will be based on reports prepared by the school – including, where appropriate, the views of teachers and other professionals who work with the child. It is part of the process of continuous assessment which takes place in schools and should include the views of the child's parents wherever possible.

The purpose of the review is to consider the appropriateness of the provision being made, in the light of the pupil's development during the year, and to make amendments if necessary. If there has been a significant change in the child's circumstances a re-assessment may be appropriate.

> At between the ages of 13yrs. 6mths. and 14yrs. 6mths. a reassessment of a pupil's needs should take place. This will enable the statement to reflect the arrangements to be made for the child:
>> during the remainder of his time at school;
>> in preparation for his transition to adult life;
>> in connection with further education, vocational training, employment;
>> or other arrangements to be made for the child when he leaves school.
>
> (DES Circular 1/83)

Transfer of statements

When a child with a statement moves from the area of the LEA who made the statement (the old authority) to the area of another LEA in England and Wales (the new authority), the old authority may transfer the statement at the request of the new authority. Under the 1981 Education Act the new authority has a duty to identify the child and assess his needs. Where the statement from the old authority was made within a three-year period, the new authority may, if the parent agrees in writing, seek advice on the child's educational needs from the old authority.

The funding of statemented pupils

Many authorities fund the extra provision required by the statemented pupil – e.g. extra teaching, specific resources etc. – from centrally held funds. In some authorities, however, the allocation of funding to meet these needs is contained within the school's budget which has been devolved from the LEA through the Local Management of Schools (LMS) formula. Each LEA will have a Special Needs Policy which sets out the arrangements for meeting the special educational needs of the pupils in their care.

What if a pupil does not have a statement of special educational needs?

If the LEA decides that formal assessment is inappropriate or the outcome of the formal assessment is such that it was not appropriate for a statement to be written; it is the responsibility of the school to make the necessary provision for that pupil, just as it is for the much larger number of children with SEN who never start on the formal assessment process.

The LEA will have criteria for identifying children who, whilst having special educational needs, do not have needs which are severe or complex and do not therefore require a statement. The criteria to identify these children will vary from authority to authority.

The Education Reform Act 1988 sets out arrangements for LMS and the delegation of finance to them based on a formula of need. Although there are differences between LEAs in the details of their schemes, most of them include a special needs resource weighting. It is through this weighting that the funding for the provision for pupils without statements is made.

It is the responsibility of the headteacher to ensure that this money is used to support the needs of its non-statemented special needs pupils. It is the responsibility of the governing body to monitor the allocation and use of resources, so that these funds delegated to meet the needs of non-statemented pupils directly benefit those pupils. Governors should ensure that, depending on the size of the school and the numbers of children with special educational needs, there are sufficient staff available with appropriate expertise, and that the allocation of staff to children with SEN is commensurate with their numbers.

The National Curriculum and pupils with special educational needs

The 1988 Education Reform Act which introduced the National Curriculum further emphasises the steps taken in the 1981 Act, stressing the importance of the entitlement of *all* children.

> All pupils share the right to a broad and balanced curriculum, including the National Curriculum. The right extends to every registered pupil of compulsory school age attending a maintained or grant maintained school, whether or not s/he has a statement of special educational needs. This right is implicit in the 1988 Education Reform Act.
>
> (NCC, *A Curriculum for All*, 1989)

Governors have a responsibility to ensure that pupils with special educational needs have access to the curriculum available in their schools, and – in so far as is reasonably practical – that the child engages in the activities of the school together with children who do not have special educational needs.

The National Curriculum Council states, in their document *A Curriculum for All*, that in both ordinary and special schools good practice in terms of access and entitlement to the curriculum is likely to be advanced where all members of staff are committed to the same aims of: providing a broad, balanced, relevant and differentiated curriculum, and raising standards for each of the pupils they teach.

It goes on to say that:

> A united school policy on special educational needs will begin with leadership from the head and governing body. It will be constructed by members of the school staff, working closely with parents, LEA support staff, health and social services, and the wider community. It will include a shared responsibility for identifying and assessing individual pupils' needs, for planning and putting into practice schemes of work which meet the full range of pupils' abilities and needs. It calls for a unified approach to setting standards of work and pupil behaviour, to recording progress and recognising achievement.
>
> (NCC, *A Curriculum for All*, 1989)

Curriculum access for pupils with special educational needs

Planning access for the estimated 20 per cent of pupils with special educational needs begins with the curriculum development plans for the school as a whole. These plans will be based on an audit of the existing curriculum. Areas to be reviewed will include:

- subject areas, cross-curricular themes etc.;
- allocation and placement of staffing – teachers, support and other staff;
- availability and allocation of resources.

As the school reviews the above issues, it will need to check the appropriateness of the decisions taken with regard to pupils with SEN. For example, the curriculum plans must ensure that:

- all staff are fully aware of those pupils who have special needs, the nature of their difficulties and how best to meet their needs;
- adequate resources – e.g. materials and equipment as well as human resources – are available at appropriate times;
- appropriate training is available to staff to enable them to identify and facilitate the learning for children with SEN;
- the effects of the National Curriculum on pupils with SEN is closely monitored and evaluated;
- a designated member of staff is responsible for pupils with SEN, with appropriate time given to coordinate the above issues.

In looking at access to the curriculum, it is useful to consider two broad areas: the learning environment and pupils' individual teaching needs.

1. The learning environment

The quality of the learning environment should not be seen as the responsibility of the classteacher alone. Influencing factors will be, for example, school policies, views of the headteacher, the governing body and advice given by the LEA.

In looking for characteristics of a good learning environment governors will need to check whether:

- there is a climate of warmth and support in which self-confidence and self-esteem can grow and in which all pupils feel valued and able to risk making mistakes as they learn, without fear of criticism;
- the layout of the classroom and building enables physical access for those pupils who are physically impaired;

- there is flexible grouping of pupils to cater for those with different learning styles;
- there is cooperative learning among pupils;
- there is effective management of support for SEN children in relation to support staff, classroom assistants, parents and volunteers. This will need to consider clear definition of roles, managing classroom space, group or one-to-one teaching etc.;
- there is access to specialist advice such as advisory, support and psychological services, speech therapy, health services etc.;
- the quality of pupils' learning experiences is managed through whole-school approaches to issues – e.g. behaviour management.

2. Pupils' individual teaching needs

Pupils with special educational needs are likely to have more complex teaching needs than their peers. They will benefit from:

- teaching which places emphasis on encouragement, acceptance, respect for achievements and sensitivity to individual needs;
- a positive attitude towards special educational needs by teachers who are determined to ensure the success and participation of all the children in their care;
- relationships with teachers which encourage them to become active learners, helping to plan, build and evaluate their own learning experiences where possible;
- a system which encourages self-assessment and emphasises positive achievements;
- partnerships between home and school which enable families to support teaching programmes wherever possible;
- teaching and classroom arrangements which take account of their individual needs. For example pupils with:
  - visual and hearing impairments may need special lighting or acoustic conditions, equipment and aids,
  - physical impairments may need adaptations to furniture and/ or equipment, escorting between classes, assistance on stairs etc.,
  - specific learning difficulties will benefit from teaching approaches which utilise their strengths – e.g. oral communication taking account of their difficulties with written communication,
  - general learning difficulties will need the programmes of study broken down into a series of finely graded, age-appropriate and achievable steps.

What are the exceptional arrangements which can be made to the National Curriculum for pupils with special educational needs?

The National Curriculum and the assessment arrangements for each key stage have been designed for use with the maximum range of pupils, including those with special educational needs. However, there may be the need to make exceptional arrangements for some pupils. There are three main ways in which this can be achieved:

1. *Section 17 Regulations or Section 4 Orders (1988 Act)* which allow the Secretary of State to modify or disapply parts of the National Curriculum and related assessment arrangements in specified general cases or circumstances. The attainment targets, programmes of study, assessment arrangements or the requirement to study foundation subject(s) may be modified or disapplied as necessary.
2. *Section 18 of the 1988 Act* which provides that a statement of special educational needs may modify or disapply any or all of the requirements of the National Curriculum if they are inappropriate for the individual pupil concerned. This ensures that any changes made will be the result of a full assessment of the pupil's needs, bearing in mind all the evidence available, including the views of the parents.

Section 3 of the statement should specify how the National Curriculum is to apply to the individual pupil. Although the statement may modify or disapply, the intention is not to make the statement negative by concentrating solely on inappropriate elements. Any modification must set out the revised provision which should be made, and any disapplication should be set in terms of the alternative curriculum to be provided – bearing in mind the pupil's entitlement to a broad and balanced curriculum.

3. *Section 19 of the 1988 Act*, which enables a headteacher to give a 'general' or 'special' direction to modify or disapply the National Curriculum for an individual pupil on a temporary basis, for a period of no longer than six months in the first instance.

General and special directions

The Secretary of State expects headteachers to use their powers under Section 19 sensitively and sparingly in those instances when it is clear that the pupil's present circumstances or conduct mean that he cannot fully participate and benefit from the National Curriculum.

General directions – may apply to any registered pupil – statemented or non-statemented. It is only in rare circumstances that a temporary exception should be considered. It may apply, for example, to pupils who:

- have arrived from such a different educational system that they require a period of adjustment to the National Curriculum;
- have had some time in hospital, been educated at home or excluded from school and need time to adjust;
- temporarily have severe emotional problems (perhaps because of a family crisis) and need special arrangements.

Special directions – headteachers must consult the LEA before giving a special direction. This direction may be used when the headteacher believes that the pupil has a longer-term need for modification or disapplication which can only be made through a statement of special educational needs. The special direction may be given to cover the period during which the assessment takes place. Special directions will automatically end as soon as the statement is made or amended. If the LEA decides against assessment or decides a statement is inappropriate, the headteacher must arrange for the pupil to resume National Curriculum provisions as soon as possible.

> A temporary exception will not always be necessary when a headteacher refers a pupil for assessment. Headteachers should consider in each case if there is a clear case for a short-term exception, and should not assume that this will be the case or prejudge the outcome of the 1981 Act assessment procedures.
>
> (DES Circular 15/89).

The Secretary of State expects that, before giving a direction, the headteacher will discuss the pupil's circumstances and needs with his parents and teachers and consult educational psychologists, medical officers or other specialist staff as appropriate. Headteachers should normally allow one calendar month after giving a direction before it comes into effect. Headteachers may vary or revoke directions, whether general or special – if the pupil's circumstances change or new information about them comes to light. Directions may be varied in any respect other than by increasing their length.

When varying or revoking directions headteachers must give notice in writing to the chairman of the governing body, the LEA (except in the case of a general direction varied by the headteacher of a grant-maintained school) and at least one parent. They must specify dates and reasons for their decisions. In the case of a direction being revoked they must also outline plans for securing the reapplication of the National Curriculum.

Parents may ask a headteacher to give directions temporarily excepting their child from National Curriculum provisions. They may also ask for any direction to be varied, revoked or renewed. If the headteacher decides not to meet the request, he must write to the parents stating his reasons and giving details of the parents' right of appeal. Copies must be sent to the governing body and, in the case of an LEA-maintained school, the authority.

The Secretary of State expects governing bodies to hear appeals. They have the discretion to delegate the responsibility for hearing appeals to any member of the governing body, except the headteacher, or to committees of governors.

Representations should be allowed from parents, accompanied by a friend if they wish, as well as from the headteacher and other specialist staff if necessary.

The governing body may either confirm the headteacher's action or direct him to take any other action they consider appropriate within the scope of the Regulations, i.e. they may give, vary or revoke a direction in the manner permitted. They must notify the headteacher and the parent in writing of their decision. The headteacher must comply with the governing body's decision.

In order to avoid continuing dispute, headteachers need only consider one request from a parent for a direction to be varied or revoked during the course of that direction. However, they must consider a further request once a direction has been renewed.

If the parents remain dissatisfied, they may make representations:

- in the case of LEA-maintained schools, under arrangements made by the LEA under Section 23 of the 1988 Education Reform Act;
- in the case of grant-maintained schools, under arrangements made by the governing body in accordance with the school's articles of government.

Under Section 19 (1988 Act) directions are not intended to provide long-term exceptions from the National Curriculum provisions. There may, however, be cases where the original expectation that a pupil would be able to return to the full curriculum is not fulfilled. In such cases, headteachers may renew a general direction on up to two occasions for a further three calendar months in each case. Before doing so, they must obtain the written consent of three members of the governing body. On the second occasion the headteacher of an LEA-maintained school must also obtain the authority's prior written consent. Directions may not be renewed for a third time.

In the case of special directions – if after six months the LEA has neither made nor amended a statement, nor informed the headteacher that it does not intend to do so, the headteacher may renew the special direction once. Any direction will cease to have effect if a pupil changes school. It is for the headteacher of any school to which the pupil transfers to judge the pupil's needs and make provision accordingly.

Headteachers are not expected to give Section 19 directions excepting pupils if:

- they are absent from school due to short-term illness or holidays;
- they are receiving education because they have been temporarily excluded from school.

The Secretary of State would expect the school and, if it is LEA-maintained, the local education authority, to work within the relevant provisions to secure the resolution of such cases.

At the yearly review of SEN provision in schools, governing bodies should be advised of any modifications and disapplications which are applied to pupils. The Education Regulations 1989 require governing bodies to provide details, in a particular format, by 30th June each year of pupils for whom directions have been given. Such details are to be sent to the LEA (for LEA-maintained schools) or the Secretary of State (for grant-maintained schools). LEAs are required to send copies of the information they receive to the Secretary of State by 30th September.

What can governors do to fulfil their legal responsibilities with regard to special educational needs?

You may find the following checklist helpful in attempting to deal with your responsibilities.

Has the governing body:

1. appointed a governor, or group of governors, to take a specific interest in and oversee special educational needs?
2. become familiar with the LEA's policy on special educational needs?
3. ensured that the school has a policy for:
   - identifying children with special educational needs?

- taking action to meet childrens' needs as a result of the identification?
4. checked that resources for SEN are adequate and monitored the allocation of such resources?
5. ensured that there is a regular check that all children participate fully in the curriculum?
6. appointed a teacher with responsibility for special needs?
7. ensured that special educational needs is recognised in the plan for staff training?
8. ensured that admissions policies do not discriminate against pupils with special needs?
9. considered that the school building is accessible for those children with physical impairments?
10. ensured that parents are informed and involved in their child's progress, or lack of it?
11. carried out an annual review of SEN provision?

How can governors ensure the school is meeting the needs of children with special educational needs?

You may find the following checklist useful in helping you respond to this question.

1. Is there a whole-school policy for special educational needs?
2. Is there a member of staff responsible for special needs with sufficient time allowed to carry out their duties?
3. Is there a system for identifying children with special educational needs?
4. In planning the curriculum, do staff take account of those children with SEN?
5. Are sufficient resources in terms of staff and equipment allocated to meet special needs?
6. Is there a nominated 'responsible person' for seeing that all teachers know about a child's special needs?
7. Does the staff include any teachers who have had additional training in SEN?
8. Is there a system to ensure that all staff are aware that their teaching must take account of children with special needs?
9. Does the school have a system for obtaining help from outside agencies when this is needed?

10. Are parents kept fully involved and informed about the steps that are taken by the school to meet their child's educational needs?
11. Is there a system for referring children who may need a statement of special educational needs?
12. Is there a system for monitoring and reviewing annually those children with statements of special educational needs?
13. Are there any pupils with modifications or disapplications to their curriculum entitlement?

Parents' rights

In February 1991 the Government issued a parent's Charter Guide, *Children with Special Needs*. The guide explains to parents of children with special needs their rights concerning their child's education and how to exercise them. It deals with the complex procedures that LEAs need to use for making assessments and statements of children's special needs.

The 1981 Education Act requires the LEA to keep parents fully informed and involved if it is necessary for the authority to assess the educational needs of a child. Parents may request an assessment, though not necessarily a formal assessment. The LEA has a duty to comply with the request unless in its opinion the request is unreasonable.

In the first instance the authority must notify the parents that it proposes to make an assessment. Parents have the right to:

- be given the name of an officer of the LEA from whom they can obtain information about the procedure;
- make representations about the proposal to assess within a twenty-nine day period;
- give information to be taken into account during the assessment process.

If the authority does decide to make an assessment, it must notify the parents, giving reasons. If at this or at any other point the authority decides not to proceed, it must also inform the parents in writing. Parents have a legal duty to present their child for assessment.

As a result of the assessment the authority may or may not write a statement of special educational needs. If the decision is:

- not to write a statement, the authority must inform the parents that they have the right of appeal to the Secretary of State.
- to write a statement, parents must receive a draft statement together with copies of all documents relating to the assessment as well as notice of their rights to appeal. Parents are asked to reply within fifteen days of receiving the draft statement and may make written comments or may request to see an officer of the LEA.

Within a further fifteen days parents may ask for other meetings to discuss professional advice. For example, in the case of concern about a particular report, they may ask to see the person who wrote that report. Within a final fifteen days from the last meeting parents may make a further representation to the authority.

If there is a continued concern about the statement, parents have the right of appeal, in writing, to a local appeal committee, which can confirm the statement or ask the LEA to reconsider. The parents have a further right of appeal to the Secretary of State.

Government proposals

The Government intends to introduce legislation to amend the 1981 Education Act. It anticipates that the provisions set out in the Bill will be implemented by autumn 1994. The aim of the legislation is to:

- extend the rights of parents of a child with a statement to state their school preference;
- establish the duty of the governors of a maintained school named in a child's statement to admit that child;
- reduce the time taken by LEAs in making assessments and statements of special educational needs;
- make parents' rights to appeal more coherent, and to extend those rights;
- establish an independent tribunal which would replace the jurisdiction of both the Secretary of State and appeal committees under the Education Act 1981.

The Government also proposes to issue further guidance for local education authorities on the criteria which authorities should bear in mind when determining which children should be assessed under Section 5 of the Education Act, and – subsequent to that assessment – for which children they should determine the provision.

Summary

In their most simple form, the aims in meeting children's special educational needs can be reduced to two general statements:
- to make provision which is appropriate to an individual child's needs:
- to protect the rights of the child and of those concerned in and affected by the making of the provision.

The processes involved in achieving the above aims would seem to include the following:
- becoming aware of a child's special needs;
- understanding the nature of the needs;
- deciding on and making appropriate provision to meet those needs;
- evaluating the effectiveness of the provision.

(*Meeting Special Educational Needs: the 1981 Education Act and its implications*)

Further reading

The Education Act 1981, London, HMSO.
The Education Reform Act 1988, London, HMSO.
Special Education Needs 1978 (The Warnock Report), London, HMSO.
Guideline 2: A Curriculum for All, 1989, National Curriculum Council.
DES, 1992, *Parents' Charter: Children with Special Educational Needs*, London, HMSO.
DES, 1983, *Assessment and Statements of Special Educational Needs*, Circular 1/83.
DES, 1989, *The Education Reform Act: Temporary Exceptions from the National Curriculum*, Circular 15/89.
Meeting Special Educational Needs: the 1981 Act and its implications, John Welton, University of London Institute of Education.

The author acknowledges the contribution to this chapter of Mrs Irene Punt, Special Education Support Team, Hereford and Worcester LEA.

Glossary

CAPITATION ALLOWANCE	Money for teaching and learning materials allocated by LEAs on the basis of numbers of pupils in different age groups. This system is being replaced as Local Management of Schools (LMS) takes effect.
CONTINUITY AND PROGRESSION	Appropriate sequencing of learning which builds on previous learning to develop pupils' capabilities.
DIFFERENTIATION	The matching of work to the differing capabilities of individuals and groups of pupils.
DISAPPLICATION	Arrangement for lifting part or all of the National Curriculum requirements for individual pupils.
EDUCATIONAL PSYCHOLOGIST	A psychologist who specialises in the study of learning difficulties.
ELTON REPORT	Report produced by the Elton Committee (Chair: Lord Elton) on school discipline.
EXCLUSION	Exclusion of a pupil from a school either for a fixed term (temporary exclusion) or indefinitely (permanent exclusion) on grounds of behaviour causing difficulties for others.
FORMAL ASSESSMENT	An assessment carried out by an LEA of a child's special educational needs under Section 5 of the 1981 Education Act to gauge whether a child requires a statement.
LEARNING DIFFICULTY	A child has a learning difficulty if he/she has significantly greater difficulty in learning than most children of the same age, or a disability which prevents or hinders him/her from making use of the

educational facilities generally on offer for children of the same age.

LOCAL MANAGEMENT OF SCHOOLS The arrangements by which LEAs delegate to individual schools responsibility for financial and other aspects of management.

NATIONAL CURRICULUM The core and foundation subjects and their associated attainment targets, programmes of study and assessment arrangements.

OFSTED Office for Standards in Education.

RECORD OF ACHIEVEMENT Cumulative record of a pupil's academic, personal and social development.

SCHOOL DEVELOP-MENT PLAN A plan drawn up by a school to highlight developments in curriculum, organisation, staffing and resources, over a defined period.

SPECIAL EDUCATIONAL NEEDS Refers to pupils who for a variety of reasons – intellectual, physical, emotional – need extra support for their learning.

SPECIAL SCHOOLS Schools providing specialist teaching for children with special educational needs (including physical needs). All children at a special school must have a statement.

STATEMENTING Provision of statements of special education need under the 1981 Education Act to ensure appropriate provision for pupils formally assessed as requiring specialist help.

SUPPORT TEACHER Teachers, often with expertise in teaching pupils with special needs who give additional support in the classroom.

UNIT Mainstream schools may contain special units from which children with special needs receive specialist help and support.

WARNOCK REPORT The recommendations of an official committee of enquiry chaired by Baroness Warnock which formed the basis of the 1981 Act which governs the rights of children with special needs and the duties of governors, schools and LEAs in respect of such children.